**THIS PLANNER BELONGS TO:

7

HABITS

**12 MONTHS OF
FOCUS, GROWTH
& BALANCE**

UNION
SQUARE
& CO.

NEW YORK

"Habits are powerful factors
in our lives. Because they are
consistent, often unconscious
patterns, they constantly, daily,
express our character and
produce our effectiveness."

—Stephen R. Covey

Welcome to *The 7 Habits Daily Planner.* In this planner, you'll find:

- a year's worth of monthly calendars and weekly pages for planning, checking in with yourself, and structuring your goals on a short-term and long-term basis;

- lessons from *The 7 Habits of Highly Effective People*, including prompts and exercises specific to each of the 7 Habits;

- pages for reflecting on and visualizing future achievements and shaping your personal paradigms.

Use this planner on its own or in conjunction with *The 7 Habits of Highly Effective People*. Either one is a great way to internalize the lessons of each habit and also to create a physical space for taking an inside-out approach to the material.

1
Be
Proactive®
2
Begin
with the End
in Mind®
3
Put
First Things
First®
4
Think
Win-Win®
5
Seek First
to Understand,
Then to Be
Understood®
6
Synergize®
7
Sharpen
the Saw®
THE
7 HABITS
OF HIGHLY
EFFECTIVE
PEOPLE

How to Use This Planner

This planner is designed to be your companion on a yearlong journey of personal growth through the 7 Habits. Each month, you'll focus on a new habit, with guided reflections and prompts to help you apply its principles to your daily life. At the start of each month, set your intentions and review the habit in focus. Each week, use the planning pages to track your goals, celebrate your progress, and reflect on how you're incorporating the habit into your routines and relationships. Every day, jot down insights, actions, or moments when you practiced (or struggled with) the habit.

Approach this planner not just as a learner, but as a teacher. Look for lessons you can share with others, and write them down as you go. By actively engaging with the material and applying the habits regularly, you'll not only see growth in yourself over the year, but may also inspire those around you.

JANUARY

Getting Started

The 7 Habits of Highly Effective People embodies many of the fundamental principles of human effectiveness. These habits are basic; they are primary. They represent the internalization of correct principles upon which enduring happiness and success are based.

But before we can really understand these 7 Habits, we need to understand our own "paradigms" and how to make a "paradigm shift."

A NOTE ON YOUR PLANNER'S LAYOUT
We've designed this planner with a simple four-week layout for each month to help you focus and stay organized. This streamlined design means the planner covers 48 weeks of the year, not the full 52. We encourage you to use the Reflection pages to capture the remaining weeks. We hope this planner helps you on your journey to a more intentional life!

HABITS IN ACTION

Take the first month of this year to consider the way you "see" the world—not in terms of your visual sense of sight, but in terms of perceiving, understanding, interpreting.

JANUARY

YEAR:

SA

SU

PRIORITIES

OTHER TASKS

NOTES

JANUARY

GETTING STARTED CHALLENGE:

It's a brand new year. Write your reflections on the world as you see it this week.

JANUARY

GETTING STARTED CHALLENGE:

How does your view of "the way things are" differ from "the way things should be"?

JANUARY

GETTING STARTED CHALLENGE:

This week, describe a situation where you see things differently than someone else in your life does. How do you think conditioning has affected each of your perceptions?

JANUARY

GETTING STARTED CHALLENGE:

This week, take the time to reconsider your reading of a situation. If you saw it from a different perspective, would your interpretation of it change?

REFLECTIONS

FEBRUARY

Getting Started: Growth and Change

Throughout life, there are sequential stages of growth and development. A child learns to turn over, to sit up, to crawl, and then to walk and run. Each step is important, and each one takes time. No step can be skipped. This is true in all phases of life, in all areas of development. It is true with individuals, with marriages, with families, and with organizations.

HABITS IN ACTION

This month, give yourself the space to change in a substantial way, solving the chronic underlying problems and focusing on the principles that bring long-term results.

FEBRUARY

M	T	W	TH	F

YEAR:

SA **SU**

PRIORITIES

- ☐ _______________
- ☐ _______________
- ☐ _______________
- ☐ _______________
- ☐ _______________

OTHER TASKS

- ☐ _______________
- ☐ _______________
- ☐ _______________
- ☐ _______________

NOTES

FEBRUARY

GROWTH AND CHANGE CHALLENGE:

Private Victory refers to the internal growth and mastery that comes from practicing the first three habits, where you develop character, responsibility, and self-leadership. What is a Private Victory you'd like to achieve this week?

FEBRUARY

GROWTH AND CHANGE CHALLENGE:

Last week you worked on achieving a Private Victory. When you move to Habits 4 through 6, you are working on Public Victory, where you learn to work effectively with others. What Public Victory would you like that Private Victory to lead to?

FEBRUARY

GROWTH AND CHANGE CHALLENGE:

What things do you wish you could *have* ("I want to *have* a better job")? This week, work on changing those wishes to "be" statements ("I want to *be* more responsible").

FEBRUARY

GROWTH AND CHANGE CHALLENGE:

Think about an issue around which you would like a change to happen on an organizational or global level. How can you begin that process yourself, rather than waiting for change to come from outside yourself?

MARCH

Habit 1: Be Proactive

The first three habits are known as the habits of Private Victory—their net effect will be significantly increased self-confidence. You will come to know yourself in a deeper, more meaningful way—your nature, your deepest values, and your unique contribution capacity. As you live your values, your sense of identity, integrity, control, and inner-directedness will infuse you with both exhilaration and peace. You will define yourself from within, rather than by people's opinions or by comparison with others.

HABITS IN ACTION

Test the principle of proactivity for thirty days. Simply try it and see what happens. Make small commitments and keep them. Be a light, not a judge. Be a model, not a critic. Be part of the solution, not part of the problem.

MARCH

M	T	W	TH	F

YEAR:

SA

SU

PRIORITIES

OTHER TASKS

NOTES

MARCH

HABIT 1 CHALLENGE:

For a full day, listen to your language and to the language of people around you. How often do you use and hear reactive phrases such as "If only," "I can't," or "I have to"?

MARCH

HABIT 1 CHALLENGE:

What is a major challenge for you this week? How do you feel about it? How will you proactively take action to face it?

MARCH

HABIT 1 CHALLENGE:

Reactive people make love a feeling; proactive people make it an action. Love is something you do: the sacrifices you make, the giving of self. How will you make love an action in your life this week?

MARCH

HABIT 1 CHALLENGE:

Sometimes the most proactive thing we can do is to be happy, simply to genuinely smile. What has made you smile this week?

APRIL

Habit 2: Begin with the End in Mind

To "begin with the end in mind" means to start with a clear understanding of your destination. It means to know where you're going so that you better understand where you are now and that the steps you take are always in the right direction.

HABITS IN ACTION

Think deeply. What would you like each of the speakers at your funeral to say about you and your life? What kind of husband, wife, father, or mother would you like their words to reflect? What kind of son or daughter or cousin? What kind of friend? What kind of working associate? If you carefully consider what you want to be said of you, you will find your definition of success.

APRIL

SA **SU**

PRIORITIES

☐ _______________
☐ _______________
☐ _______________
☐ _______________
☐ _______________

OTHER TASKS

☐ _______________
☐ _______________
☐ _______________
☐ _______________

NOTES

APRIL

HABIT 2 CHALLENGE:

What is your definition of success?

APRIL

HABIT 2 CHALLENGE:

A script is a metaphor for the subconscious beliefs and behaviors that we've been conditioned to follow, often dictating our reactive responses. What is a script that others have written for you? How can you make it your own?

APRIL

HABIT 2 CHALLENGE:

Write a script for yourself about how this week will go for you. Make sure it aligns with your personal values.

APRIL

HABIT 2 CHALLENGE:

A personal mission statement is a written constitution that guides your life by articulating your core values and who you want to be. Write a personal mission statement about this week. What will you achieve?

REFLECTIONS

MAY

Habit 3: Put First Things First

Habit 3 is the personal fruit, the practical fulfillment of Habits 1 and 2.

Habit 1 says, "You're the creator. You are in charge." Habit 2 is the first or mental creation. It's based on *imagination*.

Habit 3 is the second creation, the physical creation. It's the fulfillment, actualization, and natural emergence of Habits 1 and 2. It's the exercise of *independent will* toward becoming principle-centered.

HABITS IN ACTION

Take a moment to write down a short answer to each of the following two questions.

QUESTION 1: What one thing could you do that, if you did it on a regular basis, would make a positive difference in your personal life?

____

____

QUESTION 2: What one thing in your business or professional life would bring similar results?

____

____

MAY

M	T	W	TH	F

PRIORITIES

OTHER TASKS

NOTES

MAY

HABIT 3 CHALLENGE:

What are your priorities this week? How can you organize your life so you can effectively execute them?

MAY

HABIT 3 CHALLENGE:

What can you delegate this week?

MAY

HABIT 3 CHALLENGE:

What meaningful task or goal have you been putting off because it isn't urgent? Why do you think it keeps getting pushed aside, and what would it look like to honor it this week?

MAY

HABIT 3 CHALLENGE:

Think about a situation this week where you were called upon to urgently "put out a fire."
How can you avoid the lead-up to a similar situation in the future?

JUNE

Habit 4: Think Win-Win

Win-Win is not a technique; it's a total philosophy of human interaction. Win-Win is a frame of mind and heart that constantly seeks mutual benefit in all human interactions. Win-Win means that agreements or solutions are mutually beneficial, mutually satisfying. With a Win-Win solution, all parties feel good about the decision and feel committed to the action plan.

HABITS IN ACTION

Win-Win is one of six paradigms for human interaction, along with Win-Lose, Lose-Win, Lose-Lose, Win, and Win-Win or No Deal. The foundation of this paradigm is character, which relies on three essential traits. The first is integrity, our commitment to our own values and what a "Win" truly means to us. The other two traits, maturity and Abundance Mentality, are also necessary for fully embodying a Win-Win mindset.

JUNE

JUNE

HABIT 4 CHALLENGE:

This week, did you have an interaction that you would characterize as a Win-Win? What happened, and how did it make you feel?

JUNE

HABIT 4 CHALLENGE:

Think about an interaction you had this week. Was there a way you could have made it Win-Win, or would it have been better to walk away?

JUNE

HABIT 4 CHALLENGE:

What Win are you seeking that would be harmonious with your innermost values?

JUNE

HABIT 4 CHALLENGE:

Abundance Mentality is the belief that there are enough resources, success, and opportunities in the world for everyone. Do you have an Abundance Mentality? Take the time this week to think about how you can develop or strengthen this in pursuit of your big Win.

REFLECTIONS

JULY

Habit 5: Seek First to Understand, Then to Be Understood

We have a tendency to rush in, to fix things up with good advice. But we often fail to take the time to diagnose, to truly, deeply understand the problem first. *Seek first to understand, then to be understood.* This principle is the key to effective interpersonal communication.

HABITS IN ACTION

Communication is the most important skill in life. We spend most of our waking hours communicating. But consider this: You've spent years learning how to read and write, years learning how to speak. But what about listening? What training or education have you had that enables you to listen so that you really, deeply understand another human being from that individual's own frame of reference?

JULY

M	T	W	TH	F

YEAR:

SA

SU

PRIORITIES

OTHER TASKS

NOTES

JULY

HABIT 5 CHALLENGE:

Think about how your ability to listen has been informed by past experiences. What or who taught you to listen?

JULY

HABIT 5 CHALLENGE:

Today, as you're talking to someone, try to listen with the intent to understand. What happened? What did you learn? How did this make you feel?

JULY

JULY

HABIT 5 CHALLENGE:

Listen to another person this week, and try to understand the situation from their point of view. Compare what you heard with your initial assumptions. How valid were those assumptions? Did you really understand this individual's perspective?

AUGUST

Habit 6: Synergize

What is *synergy*? Simply defined, it means that the whole is greater than the sum of its parts. It means that the relationship that the parts have with each other is a part in and of itself. It is not only a part, but the most catalytic, the most empowering, the most unifying, and the most exciting part.

HABITS IN ACTION

When you communicate synergistically, you are simply opening your mind and heart and expressions to new possibilities, new alternatives, new options. It may seem as if you are casting aside Habit 2 (to begin with the end in mind), but in fact you're doing the opposite— you're fulfilling it. You're not sure how things will work out or what the end will look like, but you do have an inward sense of excitement and security and adventure, believing that it will be significantly better than it was before.

AUGUST

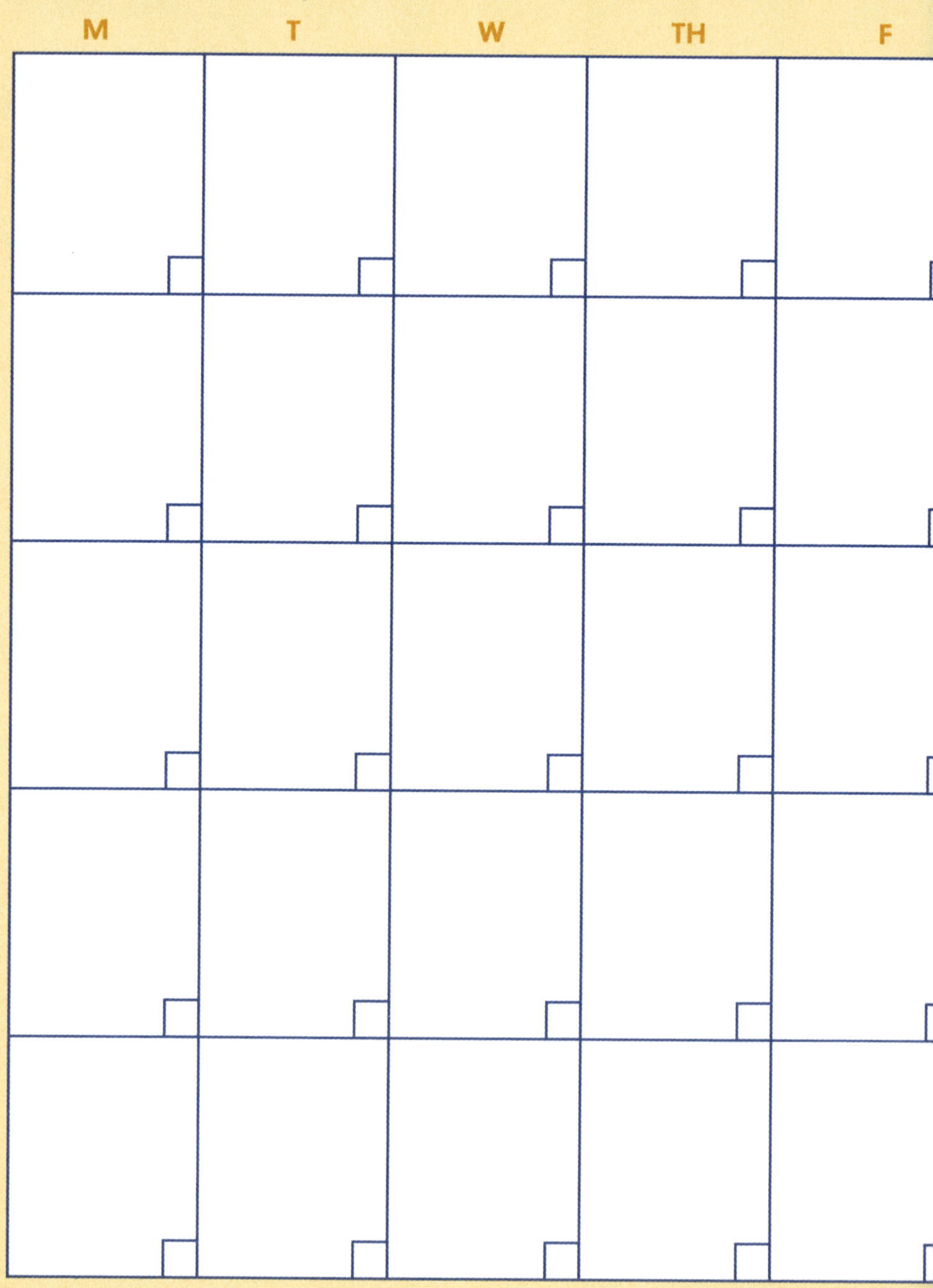

YEAR:

SA

SU

PRIORITIES

OTHER TASKS

NOTES

AUGUST

HABIT 6 CHALLENGE:

Think back to Habit 2 (or even flip back to the pages you filled out earlier this year). How do you feel that communicating synergistically differs from "beginning with the end in mind"?

AUGUST

HABIT 6 CHALLENGE:

Have you had an interaction this week that could be improved with synergistic communication?

AUGUST

HABIT 6 CHALLENGE:

This week, try communicating as your most authentic self to see what happens!

AUGUST

HABIT 6 CHALLENGE:

Approach a friend, family member, or colleague for a brainstorming session. Plan a new project, work through a problem, or create a mission statement together.

SEPTEMBER

Habit 7: Sharpen the Saw

Habit 7 is taking time to sharpen the saw. It surrounds the other habits on the 7 Habits paradigm because it is the habit that makes all the others possible. Habit 7 is preserving and enhancing the greatest asset you have—you.

HABITS IN ACTION

Habit 7 is about renewing the four dimensions of your nature—physical, spiritual, mental, and social/emotional.

- **PHYSICAL:** exercise, nutrition, stress management

- **MENTAL:** reading, visualizing, planning, writing

- **SPIRITUAL:** value clarification and commitment, study and meditation

- **SOCIAL/EMOTIONAL:** service, empathy, synergy, intrinsic security

SEPTEMBER

M	T	W	TH	F

YEAR:

SA

SU

PRIORITIES

☐
☐
☐
☐
☐

OTHER TASKS

☐
☐
☐
☐

NOTES

SEPTEMBER

HABIT 7 CHALLENGE:

This week, take some time for renewal. What does that mean to you?

SEPTEMBER

HABIT 7 CHALLENGE:

This week, express your physical motivations with an activity that will help you improve your endurance, flexibility, and/or strength.

SEPTEMBER

HABIT 7 CHALLENGE:

This week, take time for spiritual renewal, whether by meditating, praying, or simply immersing yourself in great literature or music.

SEPTEMBER

HABIT 7 CHALLENGE:

Practice an activity that will exercise your mental dimension. That could be reading a new book, beginning to learn a new language, or researching and then signing up for a class.

REFLECTIONS

OCTOBER

The 8th Habit

We as individuals and organizations have the capacity to achieve greatness. In order to thrive, innovate, excel, and lead, we must build on and improve upon effectiveness. The call of this new era in human history is for greatness.

HABITS IN ACTION

Fulfillment, passionate execution, significant contribution: These are on a different plane than effectiveness. Tapping into the higher reaches of human genius and innovation—what we can call *voice*—requires a new mindset. The 8th Habit, then, is not about adding one more habit to the seven, but seeing and harnessing the power of a third dimension to the habits that meets the new challenges of our age. The 8th Habit: Find your voice and inspire others to find theirs.

OCTOBER

M	T	W	TH	F

SA SU

PRIORITIES

- ☐ _______________
- ☐ _______________
- ☐ _______________
- ☐ _______________
- ☐ _______________

OTHER TASKS

- ☐ _______________
- ☐ _______________
- ☐ _______________
- ☐ _______________

NOTES

OCTOBER

8TH HABIT CHALLENGE:

Are you fulfilled by your job, studies, or other vocation? What would you like to change?

OCTOBER

What activity best allows you to find your voice?

OCTOBER

8TH HABIT CHALLENGE:

What are your dreams? What fears prevent you from achieving them?

OCTOBER

8TH HABIT CHALLENGE:

Make the choice to expand your influence by inspiring others. How can you inspire others today?

NOVEMBER

The 3rd Alternative

The 3rd Alternative is a principle so fundamental that it can transform your whole life and the world. Basically, it's the key to solving life's most difficult problems. It's a habit that can help you not only conquer your problems, but also build a future that's better than you ever thought possible.

If someone sees only the mental map of the 1st Alternative—their *own* incomplete map—then the only way to solve the problem is to persuade you to shift your paradigm or even force you to accept their alternative. If, on the other hand, they throw away their map and follow yours—the 2nd Alternative—they face the same problem. You can combine maps, and that helps. *But then you get to the exciting part.* That happens when they look at you and say, "Maybe we can come up with a better solution than either one of us has in mind. *Would you be willing to look for a 3rd Alternative we haven't even thought of yet?"*

NOVEMBER

NOVEMBER

3RD ALTERNATIVE CHALLENGE:

Approach a negotiation this week not by trying to convince the other party, or to compromise, but to work together to find a third solution.

NOVEMBER

3RD ALTERNATIVE CHALLENGE:

Do you feel that there's an aspect of your work or personal expression that is stagnating? To add creativity to your approach, find a new person to collaborate with.

NOVEMBER

NOVEMBER

3RD ALTERNATIVE CHALLENGE:

Think about how you see yourself. How could you reenvision yourself as a more complex individual?

DECEMBER

Putting It All Together

Think about what you've learned about the 7 Habits (and beyond!). This month is all about revisiting the lessons that resonated most with you and considering how you can add them to your everyday life to achieve your goals.

HABITS IN ACTION

Think about how you were able to develop effective habits this year. How has your life changed since this time last year?

DECEMBER

YEAR:

SA

SU

PRIORITIES

OTHER TASKS

NOTES

DECEMBER

PUTTING IT ALL TOGETHER CHALLENGE:

What positive lifestyle changes would you like to bring to the next year?

DECEMBER

PUTTING IT ALL TOGETHER CHALLENGE:

What negative paradigms would you like to avoid in the coming year?

DECEMBER

PUTTING IT ALL TOGETHER CHALLENGE:

Which habit resonated most with you this year?

DECEMBER

PUTTING IT ALL TOGETHER CHALLENGE:

Which habit would you like to study in greater detail next year?

REFLECTIONS

About Stephen R. Covey and the 7 Habits

Dr. Stephen R. Covey passed away in 2012, leaving behind an unmatched legacy of teachings about leadership, time management, effectiveness, success, and love and family. A multimillion-copy bestselling author of self-help and business classics, Dr. Covey strove to help readers recognize the principles that would lead them to personal and professional effectiveness. His seminal work, *The 7 Habits of Highly Effective People*, transformed the way people think and act upon their problems with a compelling, logical, and well-defined process.

As an internationally respected leadership authority, family expert, teacher, organizational consultant, and author, his advice gives insight to millions. He sold more than thirty million books (in fifty languages), and *The 7 Habits of Highly Effective People* was named the most influential business book of the twentieth century. He was the author of *The 3rd Alternative*, *The 8th Habit*, *The Leader in Me*, *First Things First*, and many other titles. He held an MBA from Harvard University and a doctorate from Brigham Young University. He lived with his wife and family in Utah.

Union Square Gift
Hachette Book Group
1290 Avenue of the Americas, New York, NY 10104
unionsquareandco.com
@unionsqandco

Union Square Gift is an imprint of Grand Central Publishing, a division of Hachette Book Group, Inc. The Union Square Gift name and logo is a registered trademark of Hachette Book Group, Inc.

Design by Elizabeth Lindy

The publisher is not responsible for websites (or their content) that are not owned by the publisher.

Union Square Gift products may be purchased in bulk for business, educational, or promotional use. For information, please contact your local bookseller or the Hachette Book Group Special Markets Department at special.markets@hbgusa.com.

ISBN 978-1-4549-9948-5

First Edition July 2026

Printed in India
03/26
REP